FINANCIAL PLANNING FOR TEENS

Teen Success Series
Volume One

"A Teenagers Guide to Financial Prosperity"

Yvonne Brooks

Writers Club Press
San Jose New York Lincoln Shanghai

Financial Planning for Teens
Teen Success Series
Volume One

All Rights Reserved © 2002 by Yvonne Brooks

No part of this book may be reproduced or transmitted in any form or by any means, graphic, electronic, or mechanical, including photocopying, recording, taping, or by any information storage retrieval system, without the permission in writing from the publisher.

Writers Club Press
an imprint of iUniverse, Inc.

For information address:
iUniverse, Inc.
5220 S. 16th St., Suite 200
Lincoln, NE 68512
www.iuniverse.com

ISBN: 0-595-22797-X

Printed in the United States of America

FINANCIAL PLANNING
FOR TEENS

This book is dedicated to my husband Paul. You are the inspiration behind my success.

All proceeds from this book benefit the Brooks & Brooks Foundation, Inc a non-profit foundation that helps Prepare Teens for College.
Teens can register at:

www.youthleadership3000.org

Teen Success Series Testimonials

Student age 12 wrote:

This training really helped me. It got me thinking that even though none of my family has gone to college. I could break the cycle and have a much better life.

Student age 13 wrote:

I learned how to take responsibility for everything that I do.

Student age 13 wrote:

I learned that we have to be responsible for our choices and not to blame others.

Student age 15 wrote:

I am grateful to the Brooks & Brooks Foundation. I learned that it takes more than good grades to get into college. I still have time to work on my teen financial portfolio. Thank you.

Student age 14 wrote:

This training is very helpful for the future in preparing us for college.

Student age 13 wrote:

I learned how to be more respectful and helpful. Thank you.

Student age 13 wrote:

I learned how to be responsible and become financially independent by preparing for the future.

Student age 12 wrote:

I liked learning about how to begin earning money for college.

Student age 13 wrote:

This training is fantastic. I hope that this program continues to help other teens that want to take responsibility for their future.

The Teen Success Series Teaches How To:

*Build Self-esteem

*Improve Confidence Level

*Prepare for College

*Stay Focused on Goals

*Develop Leadership Skills

*Become Financially Independent

*Appreciate Others

*Start a Teen Business

*Improve Personal Relationships

*Deal with Stress/Anger Effectively

"Failing to plan is the main ingredient in planning to Fail"

Contents

Teen Financial Check-up

1. What is the most important thing to you in life?

_____

2. When was the last time you read a book on financial management?

_____

3. Do you have a Teen Financial Portfolio in place?

_____

4. What is your definition of success?

_____

5. Who are your role models?

_____

6. What are your feelings towards money?

_____

7. Do you plan on going to college?

_____

8. How will you pay for college?

_____

9. Where do you see yourself five years from today?

_____

10. How do you feel about your school?

_____

11. What changes would you like to see take place in your school?

_____

12. Do you agree that teachers should be paid more? Why?

_____

13. Do you consider yourself a leader or a follower? Why?

_____

14. What does the word budget mean to you?

_____

15. How much money did your parent(s) spend last year for your personal expenses?

_____

16. How much money did your parent(s) spend last month for your personal expenses?

_____

17. Are your parents in debt? Does it matter to you?

_____

18. Do you believe that you do not have to be financially responsible until age 18? Why?

_____

19. Where do you get your money for personal expense?

_____

20. What age do you plan to become responsible for your financial destiny?

_____

"Teens Without a Plan Will End Up Working for Teens with a Plan"

Plan A

Why Teen Financial Planning is Important

Money for Teens
www.youthleadership3000.org

Why Teen Financial Planning is Important

Most teens are unaware about the importance of financial planning before attending college. Spending thousands of dollars in a five-year period without learning the basic principles about money is an expensive way of learning about teen money management.

The average teen usually graduates high school with a debt of $2000 or more, and a net worth of zero. This approach to teen financial planning is sometimes reflected in the parents' interaction and relationship with money.

Teens are unaware that parents sometimes go into debt to make their lives easier. Many parents have credit card debt in the amount of $40,000 or more. Some parents' total monthly debt exceeds their total monthly income.

Parents are constantly seeking more credit to make sure that their teens have the "BEST". More credit equals more debt especially for parents who cannot afford it. This is a dangerous cycle that our teens experience throughout their most impressive years.

Many teens wait until their senior year in high school before giving thought to the expenses of university/college. Many teens are relying on their parents or financial aid to pay for their education.

In order to be accepted in the best schools, teens must have excellent grades. They also must have the funding. A law degree could run about $150,000 depending on the school. A teaching or nursing degree could run between $50,000 and $75,000.

Upon graduating university, students will pick up where they left off in high school, and spend the next thirty years paying off a debt that could have been avoided. Financial planning for teens is an important tool that will assist with the process of managing money effectively, and thus enable teens to control their financial destiny.

What is Financial Planning?

Financial Planning is the process of managing money in order to control personal financial destiny. This includes setting financial goals, developing a plan for each goal, and putting the plan into action. This is the first step towards securing your financial future.

Financial Planning is the easiest way to become wealthy. There are no FREE lunches. Everyone is responsible for his or her own individual wealth. Those with a financial plan will never run out of money. These individuals tend to have a budget and savings program in place and will not allow overspending.

Individuals without a financial plan always run out of money. These individuals buy items on credit knowing that they are unable to pay the amount off in full within thirty days. These individuals usually borrow from others their entire life, until learning about how to put a financial plan in place.

A good example is someone who complains about never having enough money. This individual could be on a job, with an earning potential of over $30,000 annually, and a debt of $50,000 or more. How is this possible? This kind of money management is called living above your means. If you cannot afford to keep up with the latest fashions, your friends or neighbors, then get a second job, begin a savings program, go back to school, but find a solution that will not cost you thousands of dollars in the long run.

Another good example of an individual without a financial plan in place is someone who believes within his/her heart that others are responsible for their financial destiny. This individual will spend years stealing from others, believing that they are entitled to do so. This individual is not interested in earning a living. Common complaints by these individuals are: there are no jobs, the hours do not fit my schedule, the pay is too low, and the location is too far. Excuses that can last a life-time.

Financial Planning gives everyone an opportunity to become wealthy. This is the most powerful money management tool available. Teens are encouraged to become more responsible in the area of finance. They are also encouraged to take full responsibility for their economic future.

"The Average Teen's Personal Net Worth is Zero"

Time is Money

Time is the most valuable resource for teens. Making good choices about how to use time is what most people refer to as time-management. Everyday teens make different choices about how to use their time. Connecting financial goals to personal time is a form of excellent time-management.

The best way to determine how much money that will be available to meet your financial goals is to consider the factors of time, money, and the current interest rates available. The more time you have to save, the more money you will have at the end of your goal.

Earning interest upon interest is called compounding. This is a great way to earn more money over time. Assume that you had $50 in an account earning 5% interest per year. At the end of that year, you would have $52.50 in your account. At the end of the second year you would have earned interest on your $52.50, which equals $55.13. The extra money came from compounding interest over time.

If you saved $1000 every year, and earned 10% for five years, you would have earned a total of $6715.61. If you saved $1000 every year, for five years at home, in a shoebox, you would earn a total of $5000. The difference over time, plus compounded interest is a difference of

$1715.61. This means that over the past five years, your money worked very hard while you prepared for college.

The Rule of 72, is an extremely useful and valuable tool for teens to track how long it will take to double their money. The rule states that if you obtain one percent on your money, it will take 72 years for your $1 to double. If you obtain three percent, it will take twenty-four years to double your money. If you obtain ten percent, it will take seven years.

Below is a list of questions that teens can ask themselves, to see how they currently value their time.

1. How much time do you spend watching television?

2. How much time do you spend talking on the phone?

3. How much time do you spend daydreaming?

4. How much time do you spend feeling sorry for yourself?

5. How much is your time worth?

6. How long will it take to double your current savings using the Rule of 72?

7. How much interest do you earn wasting time?

8. How would you divide your past twenty-four hours?

Time Management Tips

1. Use a To Do List:

This will give teens a better idea of how to divide their time for the day, week or month.

2. Learn to Say No:

The goal is to finish what is on your list before committing to other projects. This means completing your homework before accepting a phone call from a friend about setting a date for entertainment purposes.

3. Watch Out for Time Wasters:

This would include ten hours of television or video games, or fifteen hours sleeping in order to play catch up on the weekends.

4. Practice:

Practice developing time management habits that works for you daily. Make your goals fun so that your time will be spent well.

5. Allow Time for Interruptions:

Try to plan only fifty percent of your time in a twenty-four hour period. This will leave plenty of time for interruptions, emergencies or just to take a break from your studies.

6. Most Important:

Focus on your most important tasks. Identifying which goal is the most important in order of urgency will produce efficiency in completing essays, projects, chores and homework on time.

7. Being a Perfectionist:

This is a huge time waster. Watch out for starting a task over and over.

8. Eliminate Procrastination:

Putting your projects off until tomorrow, or waiting until the last minute before due date, is a serious time waster for most teens. Be sure to follow through with all your projects.

9. Reward Yourself:

It is very important that you reward yourself upon completion of your tasks. It is also good time-management practice to implement a reward system that produces balance.

10. Follow Through:

Begin today and follow through with managing your time more effectively. You are worth it!

Weekly
List of Things to Do
Planner

Things to Do List

Sunday   Date_____

1._____

2._____

3._____

4._____

5._____

Things to Do List

Monday   Date_____

1._____

2._____

3._____

4._____

5._____

Things to Do List

Tuesday   Date_____

1._____

2._____

3._____

4._____

5._____

Things to Do List

Wednesday   Date_____

1._____

2._____

3._____

4._____

5._____

Things to Do List

Thursday   Date_____

1._____

2._____

3._____

4._____

5._____

Things to Do List

Friday   Date_____

1._____

2._____

3._____

4._____

5._____

Things to Do List

Saturday   **Date_____**

1._____

2._____

3._____

4._____

5._____

Teen Personal Net Worth Calculation

Today's Date _____

Assets:

Savings (CD's, Regular Savings)	$_____
Investments (Stocks)	$_____
Personal Property (video's, computer etc)	$_____
Other Assets	$_____
Total Assets	$_____

Liabilities:

Personal Loans	$_____
Student Loans	$_____
Credit Cards	$_____
Auto Loan (If necessary)	$_____
Other	$_____
Total Liabilities	$_____
Assets—Liabilities=Current Net Worth:	$_____

Teen Financial Exercise

1. My current savings account balance is $_____(this is a regular savings account that earns interest)

2. My current debt is $_____ (this includes, phone, car, credit cards and anyone that you borrowed money from)

3. My current income is $_____(this includes money from your parents/grand-parents, part-time job, or teen business)

4. I plan to attend college in _____ years.

5. I want to have $_____ saved when I graduate from high school.

6. I will need to have $_____ secured in scholarships before attending university.

7. I have $_____ in my teen investment portfolio now.

8. If I had $1000 today, I would _____

9. My financial goal for the next twelve months is $ _____

10. I save_____% of all money that I receive before spending.

Points to Remember

1. Your time is worth money. Watch how you spend it.

2. Complete all worksheet assignments before moving on.

3. Stop complaining about what you don't have, learn to work for it.

4. Your parents are not ATM machines.

5. You are responsible for your financial future.

Plan B

Setting Teen
Financial Goals

Money for Teens
www.youthleadership3000.org

"Writing Down Goals Helps Teens Stay Focused"

Goal Setting Personal Evaluation

1. Are your financial goals written down?

2. Are your goals specific?

3. Do you have an action plan for your goals?

4. Do you have a deadline for your goals?

5. Will the accomplishment of your goals help to improve your life and your community?

Benefits for Setting Financial Goals

1. Raise self-esteem and confidence

2. Reduces stress in personal life

3. Wealth at an early age

5. Increased popularity

6. The ability to control personal financial destiny

7. Success with money

Setting Teen Financial Goals

The second step towards becoming a financially empowered teen is setting goals. Goals are plans that one hopes to achieve both long and short term. Goals are statements describing what a teen wishes to accomplish, based upon what they would like to experience in different areas of their life. Financially empowered teens set goals, and follow through with an action plan faithfully, until they have achieved results that are satisfying.

Teen goals should be realistic and challenging. Setting goals early will make a difference, particularly when the time comes to graduate from high school. For example, a student who sets financial goals at age twelve, will have a positive net worth versus a student who begins at age eighteen.

Teen goals should be broken down into three categories, long term, intermediate and short-term goals. Long term goals, are goals that you would like to achieve in five years or more. These goals should include a full or half scholarship towards university, some investments and a part-time job.

Intermediate goals, are goals that you would like to achieve between one and five years. These goals should include your first car, spring-break trip with your friends, a cell-phone and so on. Many teens wait until the age of sixteen, to see if their parents will give them the first financial mistake of their life, a brand new car. At this point learning about financial responsibility takes longer.

Short-term goals are goals that you would like to achieve within the next twelve months. These goals should include entertainment, video games, a new bike and any item that you are willing to work for, by participating in a teen business, a part-time job or helping around the house.

The key in this chapter, is to recognize that teens are encouraged to set financial goals, that they are able to fund, by working in some way. It is up to each individual teen to learn the basic principles of how to take control of their personal finances, and not to look to their parents or anyone for a handout.

Teens who are serious about taking financial responsibilities, understand that the most important chapter in this book, is Plan A. Setting your teen financial goals before jumping ahead will automatically increase your chances for success. Planning is a priority.

Guidelines for Setting Financial Goals

1. Consider the time required to achieve your goal:

Explanation: If one of your goals is to be able to have a net worth of $50,000 or more when you graduate high school, then waiting until your senior year in high school to begin working towards this goal is unrealistic and can become very stressful. Be sure to give yourself a good five to seven year time period to accomplish this goal is more realistic.

2. Make your goals positive and fun:

Explanation: Choose to experience goals that are full of excitement and at the same time bring positive results to your life.

3. Write out three physical actions for each goal:

Explanation: Physical actions should include: writing down your goals, reviewing your goals weekly, doing research that will help you to succeed.

4. Follow through with your action plan:

Explanation: Goals are worthless if they are just written down. The magic comes when the action plan is implemented to match your desired result.

5. Re-evaluate:

Explanation: Go over your goals and action plans weekly to help you stay motivated. If there are changes to be made, this is a good time to do so.

6. Check to see if your actions or non-action match your results:

Explanation: This will give you a chance to see which actions are producing the results that match what you would like to experience. Remember that your non-actions will also produce a result.

7. Repeat steps one through six until you are satisfied with your results:

Explanation: By following these steps, you will begin an important step towards taking full responsibility for your life.

Areas for Setting Financial Goals

1. Dreams:

—What are your dreams for the future?
—To become a doctor, lawyer, nurse, artist, actor, business manager or teacher?
—What will it cost to achieve your dreams?

2. Education:

—What kind of degree will you enjoy the most?
—How much will getting a degree cost?
—What are the costs for books, tuition, food, housing etc?

3. Budget:

—What are your plans for earning money throughout high school?
—Will you get a part-time job, do chores around the house or will you start a teen business?
—Do you know how much money you are spending monthly/yearly?

4. Savings:

—How much money will you need in scholarships?
—What is your teen investment plan?
—Do you know how much interest your money will earn?

Example of a Short-Term Teen Plan

Goal:

To save $1000

Action Plan:

-Begin plan immediately
-Write out an action plan
-Get a part-time job
-Save fifty percent of allowance and income
-Do work around the house in exchange for allowance
-Start a teen business

Deadline:

10 months from today's date

Results:

-Very happy
-Saved $1000

Example of an Intermediate Teen Plan

Goal:

To Purchase First Car

Action Plan:

-Begin plan immediately
-Write out an action plan
-Check for the lowest price
-Set a budget for your car
-Check prices for insurance
-Estimate the cost of gasoline and tune up
-Get a part-time job
-Save fifty percent of allowance
-Do work around the house in exchange for allowance
-Start a teen business

Deadline:

2 year's from today's date

Results:

-Very happy
-Bought first car

Example of a Long-Term Teen Plan

Goal:

To raise $50,000 for college

Action Plan:

-Begin plan immediately
-Write down your action plans
-Research and request applications from the university/college of your choice
-Find out what is needed
-Participate in two or more essay contest monthly
-Get a part-time job
-Mail off three or more scholarship applications monthly
-Save fifty percent of allowance and income
-Research the Internet for new listings of companies that fund scholarships
-Contact the Brooks & Brooks Foundation, Inc for more help if needed

Deadline:

5 years from today's date

Results:

-Very happy
-Raised $50,000 for college

Dream Planning Worksheet for Teens

Short-term goals (to accomplish within the next twelve months)

Goals	Amount Needed	Actions to Implement
1.	$_____	
2.	$_____	
3.	$_____	

Intermediate goals (to accomplish within one to five years)

Goals	Amount Needed	Actions to Implement
1.	$_____	
2.	$_____	
3.	$_____	

Long-term goals (to accomplish in five years or more)

Goals	Amount Needed	Actions to Implement
1.	$_____	
2.	$_____	
3.	$_____	

Education Planning Worksheet for Teens

Short-term goals (to accomplish within the next twelve months)

Goals	Amount Needed	Actions to Implement
1.	$_____	
2.	$_____	
3.	$_____	

Intermediate goals (to accomplish within one to five years)

Goals	Amount Needed	Actions to Implement
1.	$_____	
2.	$_____	
3.	$_____	

Long-term goals (to accomplish in five years or more)

Goals	Amount Needed	Actions to Implement
1.	$_____	
2.	$_____	
3.	$_____	

Points to Remember

1. Complete all worksheets in this section before moving on.

2. Setting personal goals early will help you to succeed.

3. Make your goals realistic.

4. Have fun with your goals.

5. Review guidelines for setting financial goals.

Plan C

Teen Budgeting

Money for Teens
www.youthleadership3000.org

"Teens Without a Personal Budget in Place Experience Financial Disasters as Adults"

Teen Budgeting

Many teens spend more money than they earn. Teens who use their parents as an ATM machine or a credit card, usually have the toughest time financially as adults. The only way to access money from an ATM machines is by working very hard to put money into a personal bank account. Teens who expect parental treatment from the adult world, will be very disappointed, and find out that each individual is responsible for his or her own personal wealth.

The only way to get money from a credit card is to borrow money from a credit card company or a financial institution. When you are unable to pay your account balance in full within thirty days, the company will charge interest. If you are unable to keep up with your credit card payments, this will go on your credit report and the damage to your good credit will begin. These lessons take between seven to thirty years to correct.

Everyone will experience the lessons that money will bring. Some lessons are devastating and some can make you very wealthy. Teens, who refuse to learn early, will have to learn later on in their adult life. Without a budget in place, many teens will fail financially in their adulthood.

Ingredients
for Financial Disaster

1. Procrastination

2. No Written Down Goals

3. No Savings Plan

4. Lack of Commitment

5. Spending Habit Higher than Income

6. Uniformed about Money Management Strategies

7. No Budget in Place

8. Always Borrowing

9. Using Parents Like an ATM Machine

10. Not Willing to Work for Money

Tips for Teen Budgeting

1. Organize and Keep a Journal for your expenses

2. Plan for emergency expenses

3. Identify your basic needs and wants

4. Track your income from allowances or part-time job

5. Complete the Teen Financial Budget exercise at the end of this chapter.

Teen Buying Evaluation

1. Do you really need it?

2. Will it increase in value?

3. Is the price right?

4. Does it require maintenance?

5. Is there a substitute?

6. Does it have a warranty or return policy?

7. Can you get a better price elsewhere?

Savings Record for Teens

Age	Amount Saved	Interest Earned	Year End Total
12	$_____	_____	$_____
13	$_____	_____	$_____
14	$_____	_____	$_____
15	$_____	_____	$_____
16	$_____	_____	$_____
17	$_____	_____	$_____
18	$_____	_____	$_____

One Year Teen Budget

Planner

January Teen Budget Worksheet

Anticipated Income

1._____(example: money from a job/teen business)
2._____(example: money for birthday or allowance)
3._____(example: interest from savings/other)

Total Income $_____

Anticipated Expenses

1.Personal Pay $_____(example: 10% of total income)
2. Savings $_____(example: 50% of total income)
3. Donation $_____(example: 10% of total income)
4. Eating Out $_____
5. Phone $_____
6. Car $_____
7. Car Insurance $_____
8. Entertainment $_____
9. Other $_____

Total Expenses $_____

Teen Budget Exercise #2:

a) Add up your total income
b) Add up total expenses
c) Subtract your total expenses from your total income
d) Your total expenses should not be more than your total income

February Teen Budget Worksheet

Anticipated Income

1._____(example: money from a job/teen business)
2._____(example: money for birthday or allowance)
3._____(example: interest from savings/other)

Total Income $_____

Anticipated Expenses

1.Personal Pay $_____(example: 10% of total income)
2. Savings $_____(example: 50% of total income)
3. Donation $_____(example: 10% of total income)
4. Eating Out $_____
5. Phone $_____
6. Car $_____
7. Car Insurance $_____
8. Entertainment $_____
9. Other $_____

Total Expenses $_____

Teen Budget Exercise #2:

a) Add up your total income
b) Add up total expenses
c) Subtract your total expenses from your total income
d) Your total expenses should not be more than your total income

March Teen Budget Worksheet

Anticipated Income

1._____(example: money from a job/teen business)
2._____(example: money for birthday or allowance)
3._____(example: interest from savings/other)

Total Income $_____

Anticipated Expenses

1.Personal Pay $_____(example: 10% of total income)
2. Savings $_____(example: 50% of total income)
3. Donation $_____(example: 10% of total income)
4. Eating Out $_____
5. Phone $_____
6. Car $_____
7. Car Insurance $_____
8. Entertainment $_____
9. Other $_____

Total Expenses $_____

Teen Budget Exercise #2:

a) Add up your total income
b) Add up total expenses
c) Subtract your total expenses from your total income
d) Your total expenses should not be more than your total income

April Teen Budget Worksheet

Anticipated Income

1._____(example: money from a job/teen business)
2._____(example: money for birthday or allowance)
3._____(example: interest from savings/other)

Total Income $_____

Anticipated Expenses

1.Personal Pay $_____(example: 10% of total income)
2. Savings $_____(example: 50% of total income)
3. Donation $_____(example: 10% of total income)
4. Eating Out $_____
5. Phone $_____
6. Car $_____
7. Car Insurance $_____
8. Entertainment $_____
9. Other $_____

Total Expenses $_____

Teen Budget Exercise #2:

a) Add up your total income
b) Add up total expenses
c) Subtract your total expenses from your total income
d) Your total expenses should not be more than your total income

May Teen Budget Worksheet

<u>Anticipated Income</u>

1._____(example: money from a job/teen business)
2._____(example: money for birthday or allowance)
3._____(example: interest from savings/other)

Total Income $_____

<u>Anticipated Expenses</u>

1.Personal Pay $_____(example: 10% of total income)
2. Savings $_____(example: 50% of total income)
3. Donation $_____(example: 10% of total income)
4. Eating Out $_____
5. Phone $_____
6. Car $_____
7. Car Insurance $_____
8. Entertainment $_____
9. Other $_____

Total Expenses $_____

Teen Budget Exercise #2:

a) Add up your total income
b) Add up total expenses
c) Subtract your total expenses from your total income
d) Your total expenses should not be more than your total income

June Teen Budget Worksheet

Anticipated Income

1._____(example: money from a job/teen business)
2._____(example: money for birthday or allowance)
3._____(example: interest from savings/other)

Total Income $_____

Anticipated Expenses

1.Personal Pay $_____(example: 10% of total income)
2. Savings $_____(example: 50% of total income)
3. Donation $_____(example: 10% of total income)
4. Eating Out $_____
5. Phone $_____
6. Car $_____
7. Car Insurance $_____
8. Entertainment $_____
9. Other $_____

Total Expenses $_____

Teen Budget Exercise #2:

a) Add up your total income
b) Add up total expenses
c) Subtract your total expenses from your total income
d) Your total expenses should not be more than your total income

July Teen Budget Worksheet

Anticipated Income

1._____(example: money from a job/teen business)
2._____(example: money for birthday or allowance)
3._____(example: interest from savings/other)

Total Income $_____

Anticipated Expenses

1.Personal Pay $_____(example: 10% of total income)
2. Savings $_____(example: 50% of total income)
3. Donation $_____(example: 10% of total income)
4. Eating Out $_____
5. Phone $_____
6. Car $_____
7. Car Insurance $_____
8. Entertainment $_____
9. Other $_____

Total Expenses $_____

Teen Budget Exercise #2:

a) Add up your total income
b) Add up total expenses
c) Subtract your total expenses from your total income
d) Your total expenses should not be more than your total income

August Teen Budget Worksheet

Anticipated Income

1._____(example: money from a job/teen business)
2._____(example: money for birthday or allowance)
3._____(example: interest from savings/other)

Total Income $_____

Anticipated Expenses

1.Personal Pay $_____(example: 10% of total income)
2. Savings $_____(example: 50% of total income)
3. Donation $_____(example: 10% of total income)
4. Eating Out $_____
5. Phone $_____
6. Car $_____
7. Car Insurance $_____
8. Entertainment $_____
9. Other $_____

Total Expenses $_____

Teen Budget Exercise #2:

a) Add up your total income
b) Add up total expenses
c) Subtract your total expenses from your total income
d) Your total expenses should not be more than your total income

September Teen Budget Worksheet

Anticipated Income

1._____(example: money from a job/teen business)
2._____(example: money for birthday or allowance)
3._____(example: interest from savings/other)

Total Income $_____

Anticipated Expenses

1.Personal Pay $_____(example: 10% of total income)
2. Savings $_____(example: 50% of total income)
3. Donation $_____(example: 10% of total income)
4. Eating Out $_____
5. Phone $_____
6. Car $_____
7. Car Insurance $_____
8. Entertainment $_____
9. Other $_____

Total Expenses $_____

Teen Budget Exercise #2:

a) Add up your total income
b) Add up total expenses
c) Subtract your total expenses from your total income
d) Your total expenses should not be more than your total income

October Teen Budget Worksheet

Anticipated Income

1._____(example: money from a job/teen business)
2._____(example: money for birthday or allowance)
3._____(example: interest from savings/other)

Total Income $_____

Anticipated Expenses

1.Personal Pay $_____(example: 10% of total income)
2. Savings $_____(example: 50% of total income)
3. Donation $_____(example: 10% of total income)
4. Eating Out $_____
5. Phone $_____
6. Car $_____
7. Car Insurance $_____
8. Entertainment $_____
9. Other $_____

Total Expenses $_____

Teen Budget Exercise #2:

a) Add up your total income
b) Add up total expenses
c) Subtract your total expenses from your total income
d) Your total expenses should not be more than your total income

November Teen Budget Worksheet

Anticipated Income

1._____(example: money from a job/teen business)
2._____(example: money for birthday or allowance)
3._____(example: interest from savings/other)

Total Income $_____

Anticipated Expenses

1.Personal Pay $_____(example: 10% of total income)
2. Savings $_____(example: 50% of total income)
3. Donation $_____(example: 10% of total income)
4. Eating Out $_____
5. Phone $_____
6. Car $_____
7. Car Insurance $_____
8. Entertainment $_____
9. Other $_____

Total Expenses $_____

Teen Budget Exercise #2:

a) Add up your total income
b) Add up total expenses
c) Subtract your total expenses from your total income
d) Your total expenses should not be more than your total income

December Teen Budget Worksheet

Anticipated Income

1._____(example: money from a job/teen business)
2._____(example: money for birthday or allowance)
3._____(example: interest from savings/other)

Total Income $_____

Anticipated Expenses

1.Personal Pay $_____(example: 10% of total income)
2. Savings $_____(example: 50% of total income)
3. Donation $_____(example: 10% of total income)
4. Eating Out $_____
5. Phone $_____
6. Car $_____
7. Car Insurance $_____
8. Entertainment $_____
9. Other $_____

Total Expenses $_____

Teen Budget Exercise:

a) Add up your total income
b) Add up total expenses
c) Subtract your total expenses from your total income
d) Your total expenses should not be more than your total income

Points to Remember

1. Complete all worksheets in this section before moving on.

2. Putting a budget in place will save you lots of money.

3. Check around to get the best price before spending.

4. Do not buy anything unless it's part of your budget.

5. Leave room for emergencies.

Plan D

Putting Together a
Teen Financial Portfolio

Money for Teens
www.youthleadership3000.org

"Establishing a Teen Financial Portfolio Will Increase Personal Wealth"

Putting Together a Teen Financial Portfolio

Creating a teen financial portfolio will take time. The earlier the better. Starting a teen financial portfolio at age twelve has the potential to earn about $50,000 or more before graduating high school. Starting a teen portfolio at age eighteen has the potential to earn about $2000.

Millions of teens each year are graduating without a financial portfolio in place and without the knowledge of how to create one. Plan D, will give teens the opportunity to learn about what they will need, in order to establish their own successful teen financial portfolio.

The most important factor of a teen financial portfolio is the ability to become responsible for their economic future. The items in a teen financial portfolio will have an opportunity to work and earn interest, while the teens earn a high school degree without the stress of not having enough money.

The question all teens should ask themselves is; would I like to graduate from high school without a part-time job and lacking money for college? Or, would I like to begin taking responsibility by securing a teen financial plan that allows more freedom throughout college and the anticipated adult life?

There are seven items necessary for a healthy Teen Financial Portfolio. Teens will need a parent or a custodian in order to get their financial portfolio started. Teens and parents who need assistance, can contact the Brooks & Brooks Foundation, Inc, a non-profit organization that prepare teens for college, visit us at www.youthleadership3000.org or email ypbrooks@msn.com

Career Development Exercise

1. What type of career opportunities appeal to you?

_____

2. What is your purpose in life?

_____

3. What is your career goal during high school?

_____

3. What is your career goal after college?

_____

4. What skills and experience are required for this career?

_____

5. Will this career choice provide long-term financial security?

_____

6. What are the benefits with this career?

_____

7. What are the disadvantages with this career?

_____

8. What is the future outlook for this industry?

_____

9. Is your career choice recession proof? If so, how?

_____

Possible Earning Potential Information

Dropped Out of High School $20,000 yearly

Completed High School $35,000 yearly

Some College $40,000 yearly

Bachelor's Degree $65,000 yearly

Professional Degree $100,000 yearly

Which one are you preparing for?

Preparing for College Checklist

1. Enter essay and speech contests for scholarships

2. Participate in leadership clubs

3. Attend college prep events at community colleges and public libraries

4. Enroll in college preparatory classes

5. Volunteer with different organizations within your community

6. Attend job and career fairs

7. Take the ACT and or SAT test

8. Visit different college campuses

9. Create a file for recommendation letters

10. Contact schools that you are considering for admissions applications

11. Make copies of all your applications

12. Get a tutor for your weak subjects

Items Needed Before

Graduating High School

Scholarships

Scholarships:

Scholarships is FREE money that is available from corporations, government, non-profit and private organizations. The goal for these organizations is to assist students financially with their educational studies. Thousands of companies give away millions of dollars in scholarships annually to students throughout the United States.

Most organizations will offer $500 or more to help with tuition and book expenses. Teens are encouraged to request scholarship applications early in order to prepare properly. Most scholarships come with rules and regulations, such as a deadline and what career field the company will give money to.

An updated listing of these organizations can be found in reference books, at your local public library or you can research the Internet for more information. Securing scholarships will save you thousands of dollars in the long run.

Personal Savings

Savings:

Having a savings account is another way to earn money while attending high school. The average savings account will earn one to three percent in interest, based upon the banking institution and the countries economy.

Teens can begin a savings account with $10, $50 or $100. The goal is to save 50% of all money received from your part-time job, teen business, parents/grand-parents, birthdays, allowance or Christmas.

An example would be, receiving a birthday gift of $300; fifty percent of this money ($150), should go to savings or your investment account. The remaining fifty- percent ($150), should be divided as follows; ten percent ($30) should go into an envelope that is marked "Personal Pay". This money is used to reward yourself for following your budget and for being responsible financially. **Always pay yourself first.**

Another ten percent, $30, should go into a second envelope with the name "Community." This money should be used to buy food for the local food bank, flowers for the seniors, helping the needy/poor or to be donated to your local church. The 30 percent ($120) left over should be spent on items such as your phone bill, eating out, entertainment or music collection.

Once you enter college, your expenses will increase. The savings plan during college should then be to save 30 percent of all income and put 70 percent towards your expenses. Following this simple plan will guarantee unlimited wealth as a teen and an adult.

Certificate of Deposit (CD)

Certificate of Deposit:

A C.D. is not something that you play in your walkman or on your computer. Certificate of Deposit is another way of saving. Most banking institutions will pay between 2 to 5% interest on this account, based on the economy. Certificates of Deposits are established for three, six, twelve months or longer. Make sure that you will not need the money before the maturity date.

A fee is charged to your account if there is an early withdrawal. The average amount to start an account could be $500 or more. Check with your local banks for guidelines, and to make sure that you are always getting the highest interest rate available for your money. I would recommend that teens try to establish one or more C.D. accounts before graduating high school.

Mutual Funds

Mutual Funds:

Mutual funds are investments where money is pooled together to buy stocks, bonds and other financial securities selected by professional managers, who work for an investment company. This is an excellent way to begin your long-term savings plan. Investments in this area, could earn between 8 and 12% interest annually. To invest in a mutual fund, you would need to buy units. There are over four thousand mutual funds to choose from. Each fund has its own "portfolio" of investments, its own manager and its own goal. More information can be found online or from investment companies.

Stocks

Stocks:

Stocks are investments that buy a portion, or a share of a company. Corporations issue common stocks to help finance their business start-up costs and to help pay for their ongoing business activities. This investment can earn up to 30% interest. This kind of investment is also very risky. Higher interest earnings on your money, will always equal higher risk. You may even end up losing all your money. By law, children cannot own stocks, bonds or mutual funds directly.

The solution would be to set up a custodial account, depending which State you live in. A custodian could be your parent or any adult who is between 18 and 21 depending on the State. Be sure to investigate the full history of the company. This information is available on the Internet or at your local public library. There are thousands of companies to choose from.

There are three types of stock. Common stock is described above and is the most common form. Preferred stock is more stable. Preferred shareholders get paid dividends, before Common Stock holders. The Convertible stock is a very complicated stock, which starts out as a debt, but can become equity if the stock price reaches a predetermined price.

Look around your home to see what companies you are supporting now. Where do you buy your shoes, clothing and video games? These are the perfect companies to participate in ownership. Not only are you buying their product, you are also making money from owning a share of this company. The goal is to buy a stock low and sell high. This will earn you lots of profit.

How to Evaluate a Corporate Company

1. Research the name of the company on the Internet.

2. Visit the company website.

3. Find out what types of products or services the company provide.

4. Is the company paying a dividend?

5. Has the dividend increased or decreased over the past five years?

6. What is the stock's current price?

7. Are the sales higher than last year?

8. Who are the board of directors and what are their positions in the community?

9. What is the fifty-two week high and low for this stock?

10. Have the company sales increased over the last five years?

11. Request the latest annual and quarterly company report.

12. Repeat this procedure with each company before investing.

How to Read the Stock Listing Section of the Newspaper

52 weeks Hi Lo: This is the stocks highest and lowest value in the last 52 weeks

Stock: This is the name of the company (example General Electric)

SYM: This is the ticker symbol or letters of a stock for trading (example GE)

DIV: This is the cash value per share of the anticipated yearly dividend.

YLD %: The percent yield lets you know what dividend you get as a percentage of the current price of the stock

PE: This is the price-earning (PE) ratio. The price of a share of stock, divided by the corporation's earnings per share of stock outstanding over the last twelve months.

Vol 100's: This is the number of shares traded by the company for that day in multiples of 100.

Close: This is the price of an individual share at the market's close the previous day.

Part-Time Job

Part-Time Job:

Getting a part-time job in your community is an excellent way to add more money to your portfolio. This action will teach teens about the responsibilities that come with money. It will also give teens another opportunity to increase their personal wealth.

A part-time job, could earn $300 or more monthly in extra income. Begin your research, by seeking out the companies in your community that you would like to work for. When selecting a part-time job, make sure that it is a job that you will enjoy and have fun doing. A part-time job can provide long-term work experience for the future.

Volunteer work is also an excellent opportunity to acquire professional skills and receive free training. Volunteering can help prepare you for your part-time job. Volunteering provides training in areas such as retailing, managing, team leadership and much more. Developing these skills early will help to increase your salary potential in other types of work situations.

Job Preparation Tips

1. Visit your public library to check out books on job preparation

2. Participate in a job-training program

3. Create a list of things that you enjoy doing

4. Research the companies in your area that match your list

5. Pick up a job application from each company on your list

6. Take applications home and complete

7. Prepare a general resume that compliments each job position you are applying for

8. Drop off your application/resume to the companies along with a cover letter

9. Mail a "Thank You" card to each company that interviews you

10. Accept the job that ranks the highest on your list of things you enjoy doing

Developing a Resume

A resume is a summary of your education, training, experience and references.

Step One: Personal information includes your name, address, and telephone number.

Step Two: Education information includes schools that you have attended, dates and fields of study.

Step Three: Experience information should list the name or organizations, dates and responsibilities. This is a great section to put your volunteer work duties and trainings.

Step Four: References should include people who can verify your skills and work experience. This information should be available upon request from the employer.

Step Five: Design a cover letter. This will help to get you an interview much faster. Be sure to visit your local library to assist you with developing a winning resume and cover letter.

Sample Cover Letter

Your Address
Date

Name, contact, company name and address
of the person to whom you are writing

Dear (Mr. or Ms. Last Name)

First Paragraph
State your reason for writing. Include the name of the position for which you are applying. This is a good time to become personal by complimenting the company on their support to the community.

Second Paragraph
Give a description of what you can contribute to the company. List specific accomplishments that will connect you with the position that you are applying for.

Third Paragraph

Request a meeting to discuss your skills and qualifications for the job. Express your appreciation for the opportunity. Include your phone number and the best time to contact you.

Sincerely,

Type your name here

Sample Resume Outline

Name
Address
City, State, Zip
(area code) Telephone
Email Address

Education: Name of School
                               Expected date of Graduation
                               GPA

Skills: List what is applicable
                               Example: Focused, Team Player
                               Good Listener, Manage Time Well etc.,

Work Experience: List Job Experience
                               Give Dates
                               Describe your duties and accomplishments

Volunteer Experience: List Most Recent Experience First
                               Give Dates
                               Describe Your Duties and Accomplishments

Honors/Awards: List Academic, Sports, Work and Leadership
                   Awards

References Available Upon Request
(Create a file of references from your volunteer work, part-time jobs,
your teacher and other professionals within the community to be used
when needed)

Sample Interview Questions from Employers

1. What are your long-term goals?

2. Why do you want to work here?

3. How do you get along with others?

4. Tell us about your highest achievement?

5. What are your strengths and weaknesses?

6. Are you willing to work weekends?

7. What are your goals for college?

8. Describe your last part-time or volunteer work experience.

9. What are you hobbies?

10. Why should I hire you instead of the other applicants?

Teen Business

Teen Business:

Most teens have great ideas that they can turn into a teen business. This can include picture painting, making jewelry, design a clothing line, computer graphics, tutoring, babysitting and many more. A well-managed teen business can bring wealth at an early age.

Before starting a teen business, be sure to develop a business plan in order to guide you towards an industry that requires commitment, training and responsibility.

Teen Business Plan Outline

Step One: The Business

—List the reasons you want to start a teen business.
—Are you sure you will have the support of your parent(s) or guardian?
—Create a list to work from. (Example: babysitting, dog-walking etc)
—Choose and describe the teen business that you would like to begin.
—Pick a name for your business.
—Check to see what business and tax laws apply before starting a business in your community.
—What are the goals and objectives for the business?
—Include a bio about yourself.
—Are you willing to work on your teen business even if it does not make money immediately?
—Research books about business management.
—List your experience or background with other businesses if available.

Step Two: Service or Product

—List the products or kind of service that you would like to offer.
—Describe what you plan to sell.
—What are the benefits to your consumers?
—How is your product or service unique?

Step Three: Product or Service Development

—Who are your suppliers?
—Where are they located?
—Will you create a service or product from scratch?
—What is the process to manufacture your product or service?

Step Four: Your Market

—Who is your target market?
—What age group are you targeting?
—Describe your typical customer
—Who are your customers?
—Example: Seniors, teens, dog owners etc

Step Five: Marketing Mix

The Product:

—What new products or service can you introduce?
—What type of service should your customers expect?
—Will there be a warranty or return policy?
—What are the strengths, weakness?
—Is your business unique?

Distribution

—What types of places should carry your product?
—How will your product or service get to your customers?
—How will you handle customer complaints?

Promotion

—What are the objectives in promoting your teen business?
—To get more sales?

—To create a brand that your customer can easily commit to?
—How will you promote your teen business?
—Flyers, business cards, brochures etc.
—Where will you advertise?
—Will you create a public relations department?
—Do you like selling?
—Who will prepare your advertisements?

Price

—How will the price of your product or service compare to the competition?
—What will the profit be annually at the set price for your product or service?
—What is the cost of your product or service?

Step Six: The Competition

—Who are your major competitors?
—What are their strengths and weakness?
—Who is your direct competition?

Step Seven: Operations Plan

—Where will you conduct your teen business?
—From home, office?
—What are your goals for the first year in business?
—Who will manage your company?
—Your parents, self or a hired manager?

Step Eight: Financial

—How much will it cost to start and operate your teen business for the next five years?
—What is your projected income for the first five years?
—Create a budget for your teen business.
—What are your financial goals for the business?

Step Nine: Personnel

—What is the job description for managing your business?
—Do you have a job-training program in place?

Step Ten: Submit Your Teen Business Plan to Request Funding

Teen Business Plans are reviewed four times per year.
Send to: Brooks & Brooks Foundation, Inc,
Attention: Teen Business
6320 Canoga Ave, Suite 1500, Woodland Hills, CA 91367

Teen Financial Exercise

1. I currently have_____ items in my teen financial portfolio

2. I will start my Certificate of Deposit account on _____

3. I would like to own stocks in the following companies:
_____

4. I will begin looking for a part-time job at age _____

5. I will begin applying for scholarships at age _____

6. My long-term savings in Mutual Funds will begin at age_____

7. An idea that could be used for my Teen Business is:
_____

8. I will begin my research about investment properties at age _____

Points to Remember

1. Complete all assignments in this section.

2. Begin your Teen Financial Portfolio immediately.

3. Believe in your personal ability to succeed.

4. Share this information with your friends and family.

5. Never give up on your dreams and goals!

Questions & Answers

Money for Teens
www.youthleadership3000.org

Questions & Answers

Q. At what age should I begin a savings program?

A. Twelve would be a good time to start preparing. It is also a better idea to start younger.

Q. How can teens buy stocks?

A. Teens can purchase stocks through a custodian (adult). An adult will create a custodial account for the benefit of a minor.

Q. How much should I save from my teen income?

A. Teens are encouraged to save 50% of their income.

Q. How should I spend my money?

A. Developing your teen budget is the first step towards creating effective spending habits.

Q. What is a budget?

A. A budget is a plan of future income and expenses.

Q. What is a Bank?

A. A bank is an organization, usually a corporation that is chartered by a State or Federal government which does most or all of the following: receives deposits, make loans, collect checks, invests in securities and issue cashier's checks.

Q. What is Rate of Return?

A. Rate of return is how fast your money grows.

Q. What is a CD?

A. A Certificate of Deposit is a short or medium term interest bearing, FDIC insured savings account offered by banking institutions. There are usually penalties for early withdrawal.

Q. What is a Credit Card?

A. A credit card is a card that may be used repeatedly to borrow or buy products and services on credit. This is very dangerous if you do not have a teen budget in place.

Q. What is FDIC?

A. Federal Deposit Insurance Corporation is a federal agency that insures deposits made at member banks of up to $100,000.

Q. What is a Financial Institution?

A. These are institutions that collect funds from the public and place them in financial assets, such as deposits, loans, and bonds.

Q. What is an Insured Account?

A. This is an account at a bank, savings and loan, credit union or brokerage. The balance of this account is insured by a federal or private insurance organization.

Q. What is a Savings Account?

A. This is a deposit account at a bank, which pays interest, but cannot be withdrawn by writing checks.

Q. What is an Income?

A. Money earned through employment and investments.

Q. What is a Board of Directors?

A. A board of directors, are individuals elected by a corporation's shareholders to oversee the management of the corporation.

Q. What is a Common Stock?

A. A common stock is securities representing equity ownership in a corporation providing voting rights, and entitling the holder to a share of the company's success through dividends.

Q. What is the Dow Jones?

A. Dow Jones, are the top thirty companies that are used to gauge the overall condition of the stock market.

Q. What is an IPO?

A. An IPO is the initial public offering. This is the first sale of stock by a company to the public.

Q. Who is the NASDAQ?

A. Nasdaq is a computerized system established to facilitate trading by providing broker/dealers with the current bid and ask price quotes on over the counter stocks and some listed stocks.

Q. What is the NYSE?

A. The New York Stock Exchange is the largest stock exchange in the United States located in the City of New York. It is responsible for setting policy, supervising member activities, listing securities, overseeing the transfer of member seats and evaluating applicants.

Q. What is a Public Company?

A. A Company which issues securities through an IPO and which are traded on the open market.

Q. What is Trading?

A. Trading is buying and selling securities on a short-term basis, hoping to make quick profits.

Q. What is AMEX?

A. The American Stock Exchange is the second-largest stock exchange in the United States.

Q. What is Wall Street?

A. Wall Street is the name for the financial district in lower Manhattan, New York City, and the street where the NYSE, AMEX and many banks and brokerages are located.

Q. What is a Stock Certificate?

A. A Stock Certificate is a document reflecting legal ownership of a specific number of stock shares in a corporation.

Q. What is a Bear Market?

A. The Bear market is a name investors give the stock market when the stock prices are generally declining over a period of time.

Q. What is a Bull Market?

A. The Bull market is a nickname investors give to the stock market when stock prices are generally rising over an extended period of time.

Q. What is a Mutual Fund?

A. A Mutual Fund is an open-ended fund operated by an investment company, which raises money from shareholders and invests in a group of assets.

Q. What is Online Banking?

A. Online banking is a system allowing individuals to perform banking activities at home, via the Internet.

Q. What is a Dividend?

A. A dividend is a taxable payment declared by a company's board of directors and given to its shareholders out of the company's current earnings.

Q. What is an EFT?

A. Electronic Funds Transfer is a transfer of funds that is initiated by electronic means such as a telephone, computer, atm or electronic terminal.

Q. What is an ATM?

A. ATM is an automated teller machine at a bank branch or other locations, which enable customers to check their account balance, withdraw cash and make deposits even when the bank is closed.

Q. What is a checkbook?

A. A checkbook is a book that holds a set of blank checks that enable a bank account holder to draw money from his/her checking account deposits.

Essay Contest

The Brooks & Brooks Foundation, Inc, is offering teens a chance to win a $1000 Scholarship. Students can participate by submitting a 500 Word essay on the topic **"My Life as a Teen"**

Deadline: on-going

Mail Essay to:

Brooks & Brooks Foundation, Inc
6320 Canoga Ave
Suite 1500
Woodland Hills, CA 91367

Financial News for Teens

A Quarterly Publication That Offers Financial Strategies for Teens

---

( )Yes, I would like to receive a free copy of the Financial News for Teens

Name_____Age_____
Address_____
City_____State_____Zip_____
Phone_____Email_____

Mail request to: Brooks & Brooks Foundation, Inc
6320 Canoga Ave, Suite 1500
Woodland Hills, CA 91367

Are You Prepared for College?
Register Now:
www.YouthLeadership3000.org

"Preparing Teens for College"

Prepared	Unprepared
• Registered with the Brooks & Brooks Foundation	• Not Registered with the Brooks & Brooks Foundation
• Established Possible Net Worth of over $50,000.00	• Waits until Senior Year to Prepare for College
• Begin College Preparation at age 12	• Personal Net Worth of Zero at age 18
• Create a Teen Financial Portfolio	• Obtaining Student Loans of $50,000.00 or more

- Receive Scholarship

- Start a Teen Business

- Take Responsibility for Financial Destiny

- Leaders in his/her own Community

- Paying off Student Loans Thirty Years Later

- Financial Difficulties in the Future

Sponsored by:
Brooks & Brooks Foundation, Inc.
A Non Profit Organization
"Preparing Teens for College"

About the Author

Yvonne Brooks has been teaching, writing and lecturing to thousands of parents and teens for the past fifteen years. Her programs are currently being taught in several public schools and libraries across the United States. Yvonne has designed the Youth Leadership Training 3000 Software Program, which provides an interactive and advanced way of learning for thousands of teens. She is the creator of the Teen Success Book Series. This motivational book series will empower millions of teens towards taking full responsibility for their choices, actions and non-actions. Yvonne is also founder and president of the Brooks & Brooks Foundation, Inc. She lives happily in California with her family.

Financial Planning for Teens

"Too many teens graduate high school with a personal net worth of zero"
—Yvonne Brooks

Finally, a book that teaches teens about the responsibilities of money management and what it really takes to secure their financial future. This book will teach teens about:

* Setting Financial Goals

* Developing a Teen Financial Portfolio

* Preparing for College

* Putting Together an Annual Budget

* Calculating their Personal Net Worth

* Plus many other Strategies that will Help Teens become more Successful in life

Financial Planning for Teens is designed to assist teens in taking full responsibility for their financial future. This book is Volume One from the Teen Success Series. To learn more about the Teen Success Series and the Brooks & Brooks Foundation, Inc, visit our website:

www.youthleadership3000.org

0-595-22797-X